LOOK AND MAKE

WITH

FRANKLIN WATTS

LONDON · SYDNEY

Getting ready

Before you start, read through the instructions and make sure you understand them and that you have everything you need.

You might have some of the things you need at home. Otherwise, you can find them in most stationery shops.

Be prepared

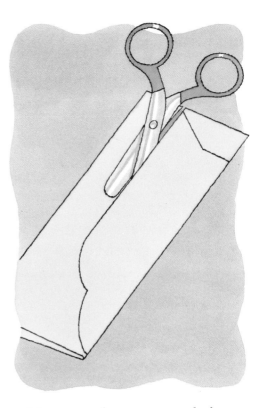

Keep your working area clean. Cover it with old newspaper and tidy up as you go along.

Always wear an apron to protect your clothes. Wash your hands when they get dirty.

Always be careful when you use scissors. If you find anything tricky to cut, ask an adult to help you.

Things you need:

On this page you can see the general things you will need for making the projects.

paint

PVA glue

stick glue

sticky tape

poster putty

round-ended scissors

ruler

paintbrushes

felt-tip pens

pencil

stiff paper and coloured card

Jigsaw

You will need:

paint your own picture
or cut one from a
magazine

PVA glue

card

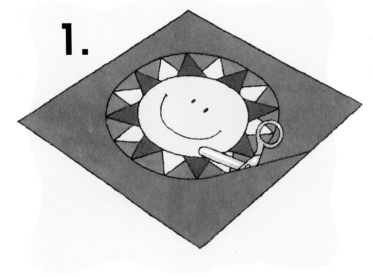

1.

Cut round your picture to
make a circle.

2.

Glue the picture onto the card
and then cut round the circle.

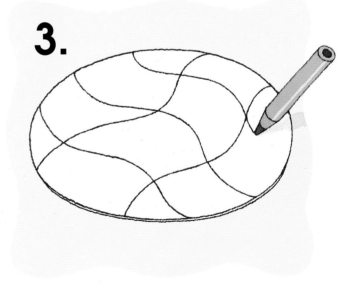

3.

Draw wavy lines on the
back as shown here.

4

You can make your
jigsaw any shape
you like.

Have fun trying
to put your jigsaw
back together.

4.

Cut your jigsaw out
following the lines.

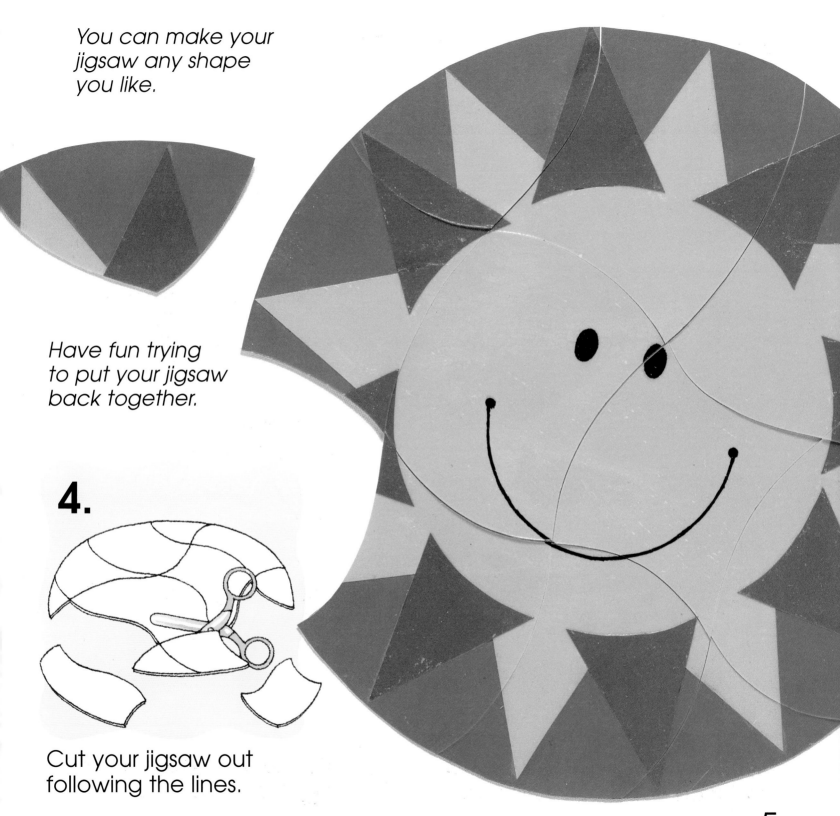

5

Bird badge

You will need:

card

sticky tape

stick glue

coloured paper

paper clip

You can make the badges
any shape you like.

Your badge
will slide
neatly over
the top of
a pocket.

6

1.

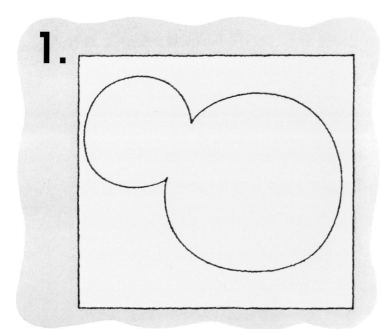

Draw a bird shape on some coloured paper. Copy this one.

2.

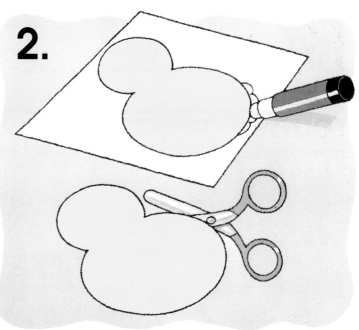

Cut the bird out and glue it to some card. Trim the edges.

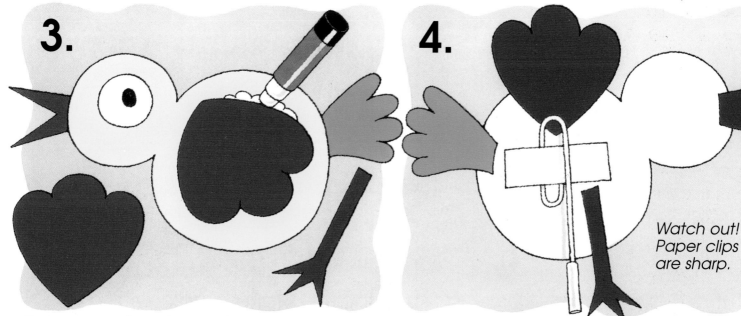

3.

Draw and cut out paper wings, a beak, leg and an eye. Glue them to the bird.

4.

Watch out! Paper clips are sharp.

Open out the paper clip and tape it to the back of the bird. Tape the bottom of the clip.

7

Mobile

You will need:

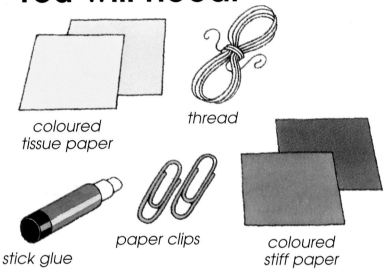

coloured
tissue paper

thread

stick glue

paper clips

coloured
stiff paper

*Hang your mobile
near a window.*

1.

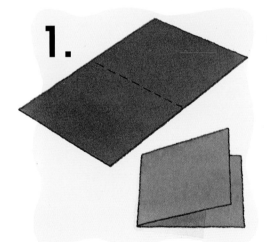

Cut out two paper
rectangles, both
the same size.
Fold them in half.

2.

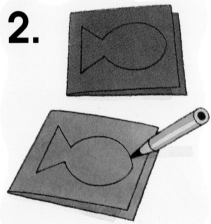

Draw a fish in the
middle of each
piece. Copy the
one shown here.

3.

Make a hole with a
pencil point in each fish.
Slide in the scissors and
cut out on both sides.

You can try any shape you like for the middle of your mobile.

Decorate your mobile by cutting shapes along the bottom.

4.

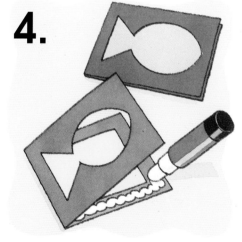

Put a square of tissue paper inside each piece. Glue the edges together.

5.

Cut a slit in the middle of the bottom of one piece and a slit in the top of the other.

6.

Slot the pieces together. Slide a paper clip on the top. Tie on thread.

9

Monster door sign

You will need:

stiff yellow paper

stick glue

thick black pen

large plate and glass, or other round objects

red and white paper

You can write any message you like on your sign.

Hang your sign on a door handle.

Matt's room

1.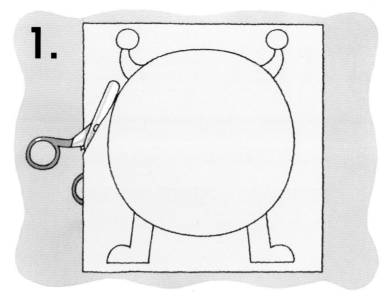

Draw round a large plate on the yellow paper. Add horns and legs if you like. Cut out the monster shape.

2.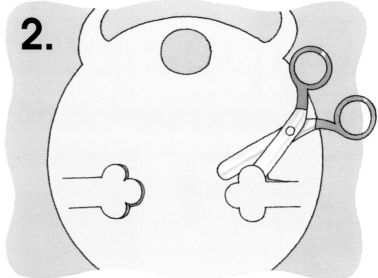

Cut out a hole at the top. Draw hand shapes. Carefully poke in the scissors and cut round the top part of each hand.

3.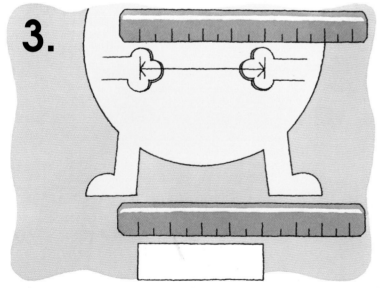

Measure the gap between the two hands. Draw and cut out a sign that will fit into the gap. Slot the sign in the monster's hands.

4.

Draw round a glass on white paper for eyes. Cut them out and glue them on. Make red circles for spots. Add a mouth.

11

Paper penguin

You will need:

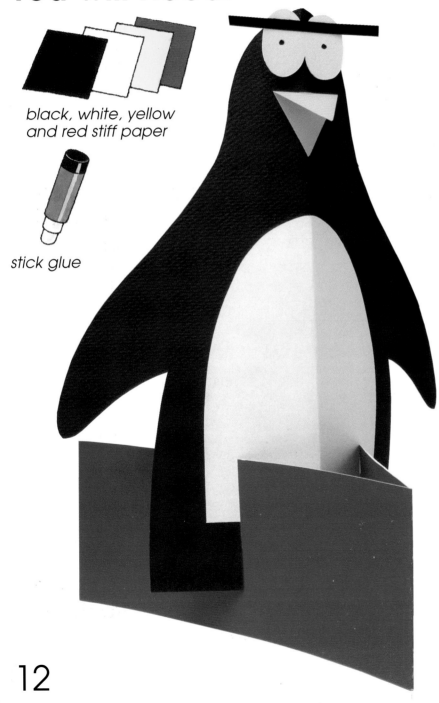

black, white, yellow and red stiff paper

stick glue

1.

Fold a piece of black paper in half. Draw half a penguin. Cut it out through both sides.

2.

Open out the penguin. Cut out a white stomach. Glue it on.

3.

Cut a yellow diamond, fold it and glue it on for a beak. Stick on paper eyes and a brow.

4.

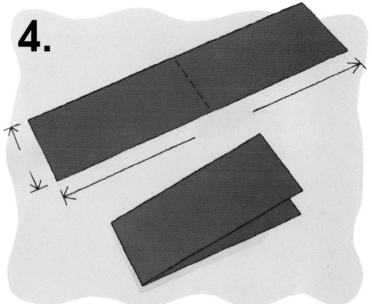

Draw and cut out a strip of red paper to the size shown. Fold it in half to make the base.

5.

Cut a slit halfway along the base on both sides. Open it out to make a 'V' shape.

6.

Cut two slits in the bottom of the penguin so it can fit into the slits on the base.

Box boat

You will need:

large cardboard box
(big enough to sit in)

large sheets
of stiff paper

sticky tape

paint

stick glue

coloured paper

1.

Turn the box upside down. Poke in the scissors and cut along one end. Ask an adult to help you.

2.

Press firmly on the corners of the side you have made the cut, to make a pointed shape.

3.

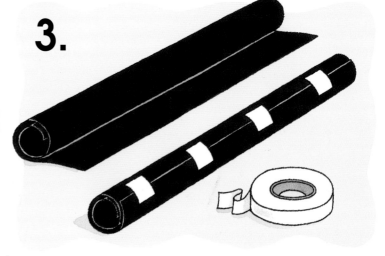

Roll a large sheet of stiff paper and tape it down to make a mast. Paint it if you like.

14

4.

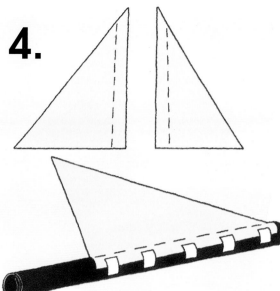

Cut two large triangles of stiff paper for sails. Make folds as shown. Tape the folds to the mast.

5.

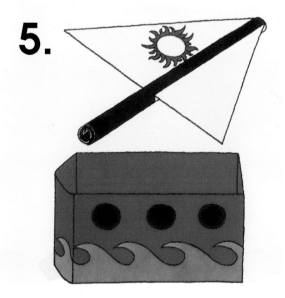

Decorate the sails and boat with bits of coloured paper and paint.

You could use a large poster tube for the mast.

Hold the mast when you sit in the boat.

15

Flower specs

You will need:

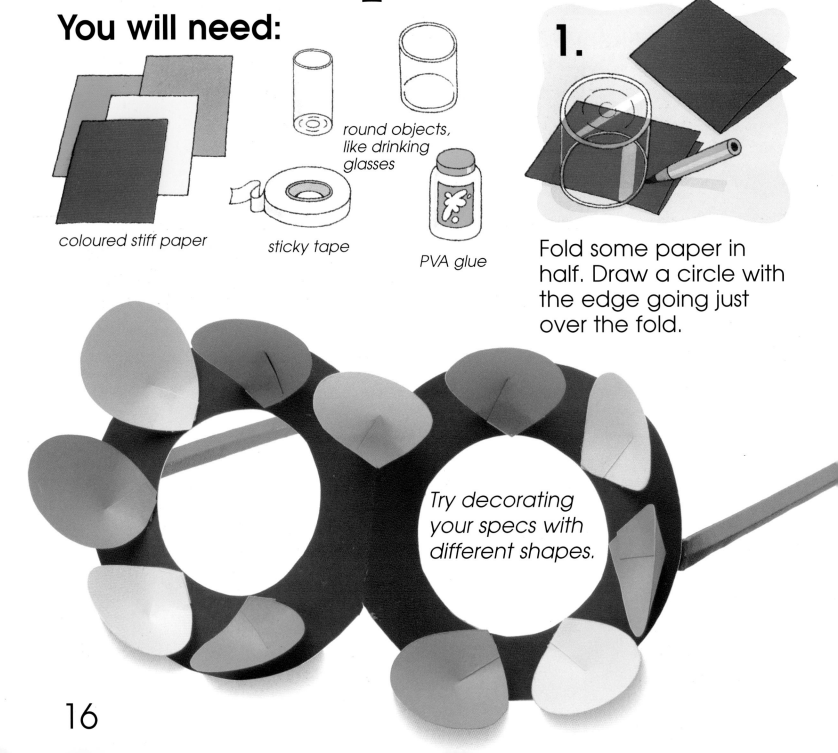

coloured stiff paper

round objects, like drinking glasses

sticky tape

PVA glue

1.

Fold some paper in half. Draw a circle with the edge going just over the fold.

Try decorating your specs with different shapes.

2.

Draw a smaller circle in the middle as shown here.

3.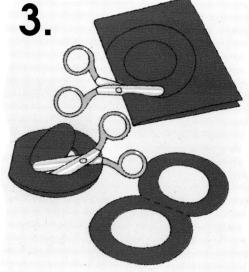

Cut round the shape through both sides. Cut out the eye holes and open up your specs.

4.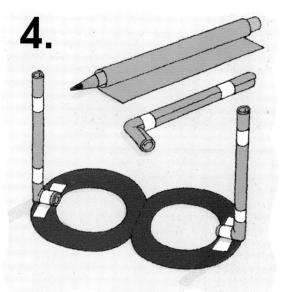

Roll paper round a pencil. Tape and slide out the pencil. Bend and tape on the arms.

5.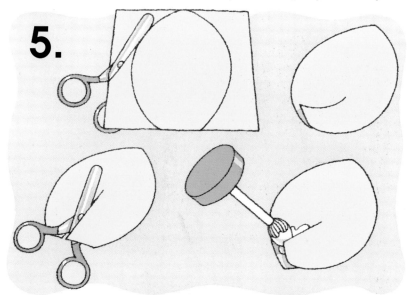

Cut out paper petals. Make a slit in the middle of each. Fold one side across the middle and glue down.

6.

Decorate your specs by gluing the petals to the front. Leave to dry.

Paper sandals

You will need:

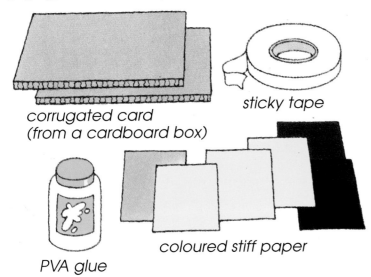

corrugated card
(from a cardboard box)

sticky tape

PVA glue

coloured stiff paper

1.

Ask an adult for help.

Draw round your shoes onto corrugated card. Cut out to make the soles. Do two pairs.

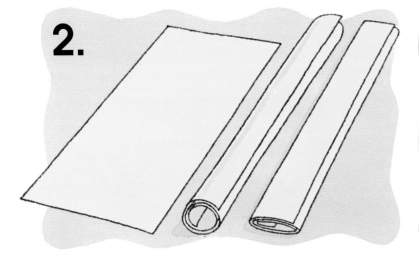

2.

Cut eight large rectangles of paper. Roll them into tubes about 1.5cm wide. Press down to flatten them into strips.

3.

Ask someone to help.

Put your foot onto a sole and wrap three of the paper strips around. Tape the strips to the bottom of the sole.

18

You can glue on a coloured paper insole.

Don't wear these in the rain!

Decorate your sandals with shapes made from coloured paper.

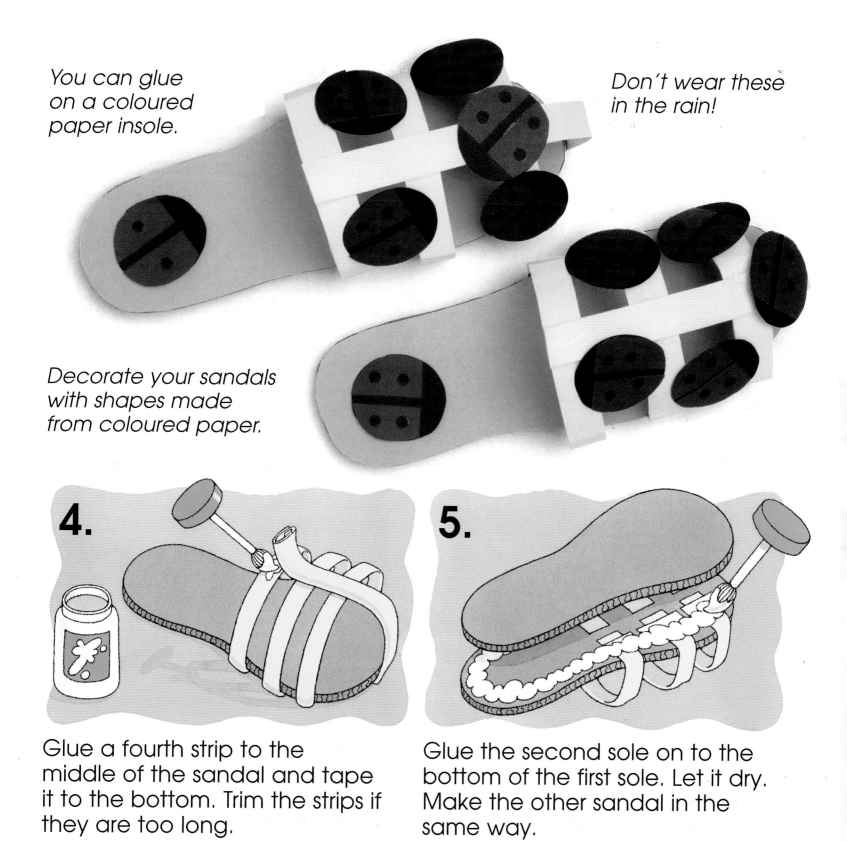

4.

Glue a fourth strip to the middle of the sandal and tape it to the bottom. Trim the strips if they are too long.

5.

Glue the second sole on to the bottom of the first sole. Let it dry. Make the other sandal in the same way.

19

Top hat

You will need:

coloured stiff paper

small plate (or saucer)

large plate

PVA glue

coloured paper

Decorate your hat with coloured paper.

1.

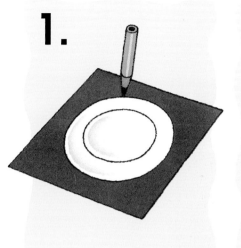

Draw round the large plate on stiff paper. Cut out the circle.

2.

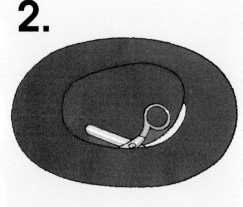

Keep the cut-out circle.

Put a small plate in the middle. Draw and cut out a circle to make the brim.

3.

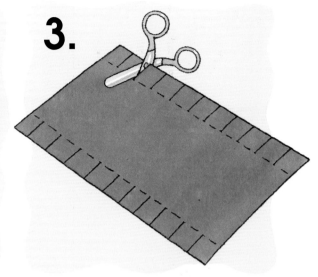

Cut a paper rectangle big enough to fit around your head. Make cuts in the long edges.

4.

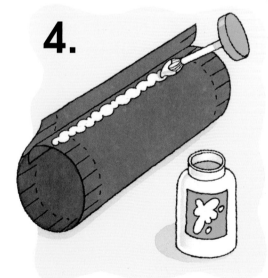

Roll the rectangle into a tube that will fit your head. Now glue it down.

5.

Push the tube through the brim. Fold the flaps. Glue them to the brim.

6.

Stick the cut-out circle to the flaps on the top of the tube. Leave to dry.

Pop-up boat

You will need:

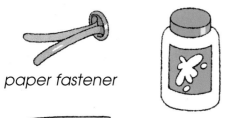

paper fastener

PVA glue

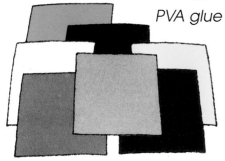

coloured stiff paper

1.

Cut out a rectangle of paper (35cm by 20cm) and fold it in half.

2.

Draw and cut out paper waves (20cm by 7cm) and make a fold along the bottom.

3.

Draw and cut out a paper boat. Copy the one shown here. Don't make it too big.

4.

Cut out a small strip of paper and fold it at both ends. Glue one end to the back of the waves.

You can glue on your boat if you don't have a paper fastener.

Decorate your card.

5. Glue the other end to one side of the folded paper. Glue the waves to the other side.

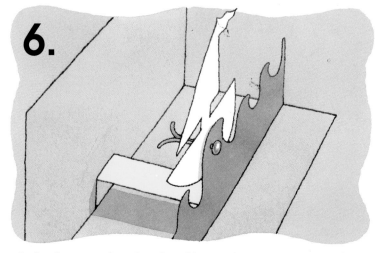

6. Make a hole in the waves and boat with a pencil. Poke in a paper fastener and open it out.

23

Space rocket scene

You will need:

PVA glue

coloured and black and white stiff paper

cardboard box
(a shoe box is good)

black paint

1.

Mix some black paint with PVA glue to thicken it and paint the inside of the box. Leave it to dry.

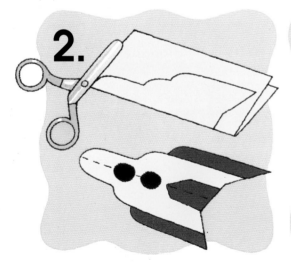

2.

Fold some paper and draw half a rocket. Cut through both sides. Decorate it.

3.

Cut a strip of paper. Fold the ends and glue one end to the rocket.

4.

Glue the other end of the strip and stick it to the back of the box.

5.

Draw and cut out circles to make planets (you can draw round coins). Decorate and glue them to the box like the rocket. Add lots of stars.

6.

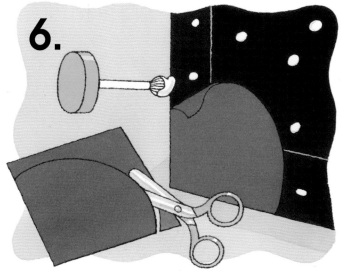

Draw a large circle on the corner of some paper. Cut it out and glue it to the corner of the box.

Ginger cat

You will need:

orange, black and white paper

PVA glue

sticky tape

1.

Screw up two balls of orange paper, one bigger than the other. Glue them together.

2.

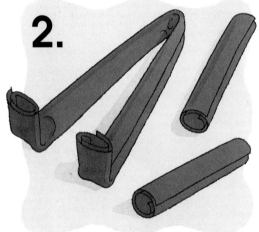

Roll a long tube of paper, bend it in half and fold up the ends. Roll two small tubes.

3.

Tape the long tube and the two small tubes to the body to make the legs.

4.

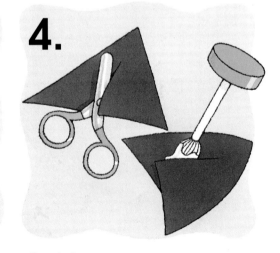

Cut two paper triangles. Cut slits in both. Fold over one side and glue down.

26

5.

Glue the ears to the head.
Roll a tube of orange paper,
bend one end and tape it to
the body for a tail.

6.

Cut out and stick on paper
eyes, mouth, nose and
whiskers. Glue on strips of
white paper for stripes.

*You could make your
cat using old newspaper.
Paint it orange.*

*Add
black
paper
claws.*

27

Puppy puppet

You will need:

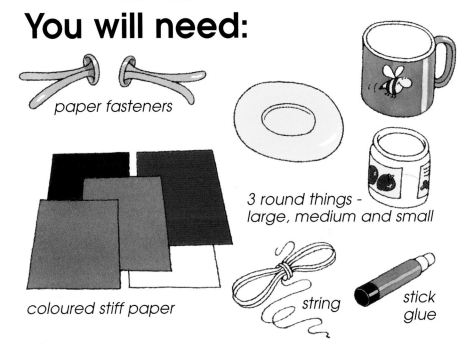

paper fasteners

coloured stiff paper

3 round things - large, medium and small

string

stick glue

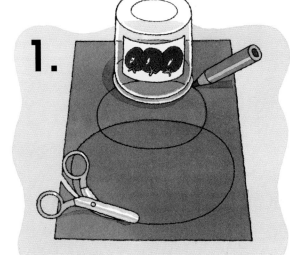

1.

Draw around the round things on the paper as shown. Cut around the edge for the body.

2.

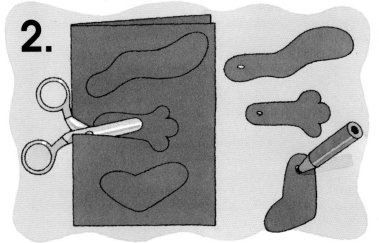

Draw and cut out arms, legs and ears from folded paper. Make a pencil hole in each piece.

3.

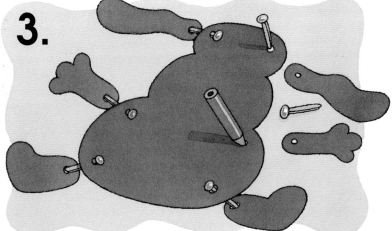

Make six holes in the body. Push a paper fastener through each hole and through each piece.

28

4.

Spread each piece out. Hook back the fasteners' wings and tie string to them as shown.

5.

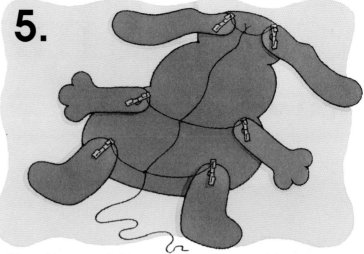

Starting at the top, tie a long piece of string to the middle of each of the shorter strings.

Add a red tongue.

Decorate your puppy with coloured paper and felt-tip pens.

Pull the string to make your puppy move.

29

Clown mask

You will need:

old newspapers

flour

balloon (blown up but not too full)

two plastic bowls

water

card

coloured paper

PVA glue

pin

sticky tape

paint

1.

Cut lots of strips of newspaper. Mix flour and water to make a thick creamy paste.

2.

Rest the balloon in a bowl. Paste strips onto half the balloon. Do five layers.

3.

Screw up a small ball of newspaper for the nose and paste strips to it.

4.

Ask an adult for help

Leave overnight until completely dry. Pop the balloon with a pin. Cut out the mask shape.

5.

Push in scissors and cut out eyes and a hole at the bottom. Glue on the nose.

6.

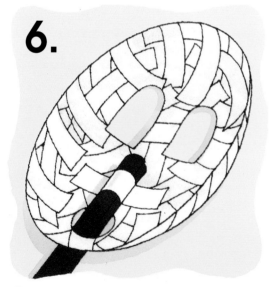

Roll and tape a thin tube of card. Push it through the hole and tape it to the inside.

Decorate your mask with paint and bits of coloured paper. Scrunch up paper for the ears.

Mix the paint with PVA glue to make it thicker.

Turn the page to see how to make this teddy mask.

31

Teddy mask

You will need:

2 plastic bowls

2 cooking apples

water

flour

PVA glue

pin

sticky tape

paint

balloon (blown up but not too full)

old newspapers

card

1.

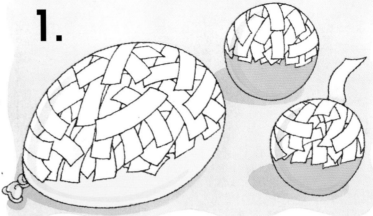

Follow steps 1 and 2 for the clown mask. Then paste strips of paper to the top halves of the apples for ears. Leave to dry.

2.

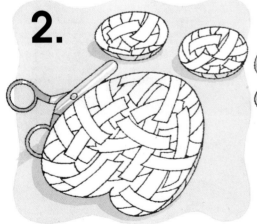

Lift the ears off the apples and trim them. Pop the balloon. Cut a teddy mask.

3.

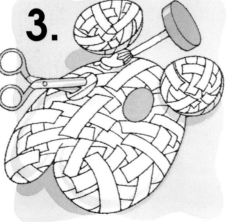

Glue the ears to the mask. Push in the scissors and cut out eye holes.

4.

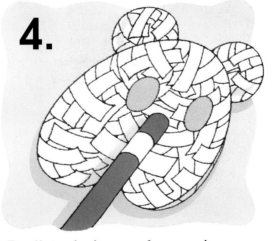

Roll a tube of card and tape to the inside of the mask. Paint your teddy.